Tracking Wildlife with Frank Craighead

By M. J. Calabro

CELEBRATION PRESS
Pearson Learning Group

Contents

How to Tag a Grizzly Bear

Wildlife scientist Frank Craighead aimed his rifle at the grizzly bear in the distance. Bull's-eye! He had shot the female bear with a drug that would **sedate** her for about 15 minutes.

Frank and his brother, John, quickly snapped identification tags onto the bear's ears. They also fitted her with a radio collar that would let them track her from afar. By observing this bear and hundreds of others, the Craigheads would learn more about grizzlies than anyone had ever known.

Frank was well qualified for this important research work. He had studied wild animals ever since he was a child.

Frank (right) and John fitting a radio collar on a grizzly bear

Most kids wonder what they'll do when they grow up. Frank Cooper Craighead Jr. never did. He always knew that his career would involve science and the outdoors.

Craighead was born on August 14, 1916, into a family of **naturalists**. His father was a forest **entomologist** for the U.S. Department of Agriculture. His mother worked for a time in a biology lab. The family lived in Washington, D.C., during the school year. They spent summers in a rural part of Pennsylvania. The Craigheads' country land had been deeded to their ancestors in 1742 by the son of William Penn, the founder of Pennsylvania.

Frank (right) and John as boys

Frank wasn't the only budding naturalist in the family. His identical twin, John, also loved the outdoors. The brothers were best friends who did almost everything together. That pattern lasted well into their adult lives.

From childhood, the boys hiked in the woods with their parents. They learned the scientific and common names of trees, wildflowers, birds, and insects. On many weekends, the twins' father took them camping on the banks and islands of the Potomac River. The area around Washington and the Potomac wasn't as highly developed as it is today.

They pitched tents and cooked their own meals over a campfire. Often they breakfasted and dined on fish they had just caught. The Craighead boys canoed, climbed trees, and scrambled along rocky cliffs. They became sharp-eyed birdwatchers. In warm weather, instead of burrowing into their sleeping bags, they slept under the open sky on sweet-smelling pine branches.

Some kids are natural leaders. Frank and John certainly had that quality. Friends liked to be with them because time spent with the twins was never dull. The boys often let their sister, Jean, who was three years younger, tag along on their adventures. Jean camped, caught snakes and frogs, and generally did everything her brothers did.

The Craigheads' sister grew up to be famous in her own right. Jean Craighead George wrote *My Side of the Mountain, Julie of the Wolves,* and more than 100 well-known books on animals and nature for young readers.

As teenagers, the Craigheads were captivated by an article on falconry in *National Geographic* magazine. Falconers train hawks and other birds of prey to hunt for small game. Falconry had been "the sport of kings" in Europe and Asia for centuries. However, the sport was almost unknown in the United States.

The brothers realized that the upper Potomac River area was prime territory for hawks. By studying books and proceeding step by step, they

Frank Craighead as a young falconer. The straps holding the bird to his gloved hand are called jesses.

taught themselves the basics of falconry. Soon the twins were capturing and training what they called "the most spirited and courageous birds alive." They photographed the hawks as well, taking slides and movie films with the bulky cameras of the era. Frank loved photography and became an expert at developing his own pictures.

Scraping up all their nerve, the brothers brought their photos and a story idea to *National Geographic*. The result was an article, "Adventures with Birds of Prey." It was published when they were 20 years old. Their first book, *Hawks in the Hand*, came two years later. The Craigheads' work revived falconry in America.

The twins had grown up hearing about the western part of America from their father. He traveled west once a year to do research. They decided to journey west as well before starting college at Pennsylvania State University.

Joined by a friend and a pet magpie, the brothers traveled in an old car packed with camping supplies and cameras. Their destination was Wyoming, where they studied the golden eagle. These huge, fierce birds of prey are native to northern mountains. The trip led to new articles in *National Geographic* and *The Saturday Evening Post*. Their articles about the golden eagle brought the

A golden eagle

Craigheads to the attention of millions of readers.

As young men, Frank and John were also avid wrestlers. The sport suited them well. Each was fairly short (about 5 foot 6 inches), muscular, and competitive. So identical were the twins in looks and personality, in fact, that they easily fooled coaches and teachers by substituting for each other. "They would never admit to doing the same switch on dates," Frank's son Lance later said.

Frank once summed up his main interest as "ecology, the study of plants and animals and their relations to one another." He and his brother went to the University of Michigan for master's degrees in ecology and wildlife management. Next, they would leave America for a truly exotic adventure.

Traveling the World

The Craigheads' magazine pieces were starting to bring them fame. Fans sent them letters. One letter came all the way from Bhavnagar, India. It was signed Prince K. S. Dharmakumarsinhji. "Call me Bapa for short," the writer urged.

Bapa was a brother of the Maharaja, the Asian Indian equal of a king. Like Frank and John, he loved falconry. When this athletic young man visited America in the late 1930s, he spent two weeks with the twins. He invited them to be his guests in India someday. The Craigheads convinced the editors of *National Geographic* that such a visit would make a

Frank and John with their friend Bapa

unique article, and the editors agreed. The magazine paid their way to India in 1940.

"What a life!" the brothers later wrote. As guests of the royal family, they lived as princes. The falconry in Bhavnagar was superb.

The Craigheads sailed home knowing that their lives would soon be very different. Since 1939, much of the world had been at war. The United States entered World War II in December 1941. Frank and John interrupted their Ph.D. studies to enlist in the U.S. Navy.

The brothers sailed to Asia again, this time to the Marshall Islands. Drawing on their talents in the outdoors, they created survival-training programs for the military. The Craigheads found that some of the saltwater isles of the South Pacific, which seemed to be **arid**, had fresh water running below the beaches. They learned how to make full use of the coconut tree for food and shelter. The brothers wrote a U.S. Navy field manual called *How to Survive on Land and Sea*.

Frank made another important trip during the war. While on shore leave, he married Esther Stevens, a fellow student at the University of Michigan. Good-humored, calm Esther was a fine match for Frank. Once the war ended, the newlyweds would make their life out west.

Settling in Moose, Wyoming

People sometimes fall in love with a place the moment they see it. That had happened to Frank and John when they explored the Jackson Hole area of northwestern Wyoming after high school. "They loved the big spaces, the fishing, the wildlife, the protected land," as Frank's son Charlie later said.

After World War II, the brothers put down roots in Moose, Wyoming. While finishing their Ph.D. studies in Michigan, they bought land in Moose. There, they built neighboring log cabins facing the Snake River and the Teton peaks.

Although the Craigheads worked as environmental

The Teton Range in the Rocky Mountains has many peaks more than two miles high.

scientists in different parts of the country for the next decade, they returned to Moose whenever they could. They spent time there on a project to find out how many owls and hawks nested in a given area of Wyoming, how far the birds ranged, and how long they lived. The brothers kept track of the birds by attaching a band to the leg of each one. Wildlife biologists do this type of fieldwork to gather data about animal populations.

During these years, the brothers started families. Frank and Esther had three children: Lance, Charlie, and Jana. John and his wife also had two sons and a daughter. The families were so close that all the kids sometimes said "Daddy Frank" and "Daddy John" rather than "Dad" and "Uncle." Like generations of Craigheads before them, the six children spent much of their time in the outdoors.

Frank and John also turned their attention to land use issues. Part of Moose was in Grand Teton National Park. By the early 1950s, more than a million people a year had begun to visit the park. How would their presence affect the animals and the wilderness? The Craigheads wrote about this question in an article for *National Geographic*. Their interest in how people and animals shared the outdoors was leading them in the direction of the grizzly bear study to come.

Bighorn sheep

Frank spent a few years managing the Desert Game Range in Nevada. (It is now called the Desert National Wildlife Range.) The range offers a protected habitat to desert bighorn sheep, coyotes, and many types of birds. There, Frank learned to use capture guns and **anesthetics** in the study of large mammals. Experience in this area later proved invaluable to his work with grizzly bears. The range was near nuclear weapon-testing sites. Frank was concerned about the effects of radiation, so he decided to find a new job in a different part of the country. He moved the family to Washington, D.C., near his childhood home. Frank loved being able to introduce his kids to his favorite camping and fishing spots on the Potomac River.

While based in Washington, Frank directed the U.S. Forest Service's recreation research department. It was important work, and he enjoyed it, but he longed to move back to Wyoming.

Frank and John began to think about studying grizzly bears. Once, these massive creatures had roamed freely throughout the West. They had been hunted almost out of existence by grizzly hunters, who used a powerful rifle that was popular in the late 1800s.

Some grizzlies did survive in national parks, where they could not be hunted. A biologist from Moose, Olaus Murie, had made a pioneering grizzly study in Yellowstone National Park. Yellowstone, America's first national park, covers a huge area that extends into Wyoming, Montana, and Idaho. Murie made his study during World War II. Since then, no outside scientists had done fieldwork on Yellowstone's grizzlies.

Was the grizzly population dying out? That question worried the Craigheads. They regarded the loss of any species, especially one as awe-inspiring as the grizzly, as a loss for all humankind.

Yellowstone was the right place to learn more about grizzlies, and the Craigheads were the right scientists to do it. They began to seek approval and funding for a study that would track grizzly bears.

Operation Grizzly Bear

In order to study grizzly bears in Yellowstone, the Craigheads had to get permission from the National Park Service. The Park Service agreed to the plan, but it did not hire the brothers as government employees. That was fine with them. They preferred to work as independent scientists.

The brothers raised the funds to pay for the study. Their excellent reputation made the task easier. Seventeen organizations, including the Park Service, gave financial support. One of the main funders was the National Geographic Society, which had encouraged the Craigheads' work for so many years.

The Craigheads remove an anesthesized grizzly bear from a trap in Yellowstone.

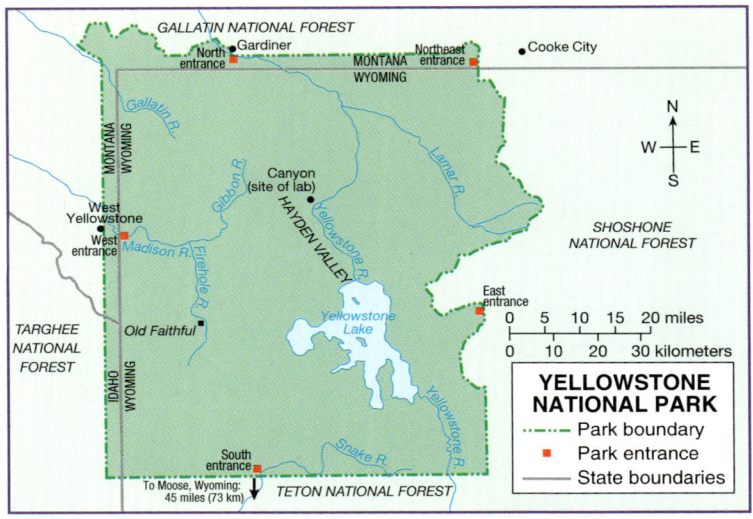

The Craigheads arrived in Wyoming for the start of the study in 1959. Their destination was Canyon laboratory. The lab was in an old wooden building near the center of Yellowstone.

As the study's base of operations, Canyon lab housed the Craigheads' equipment and files. The scientists and graduate students working on the study slept in bunk rooms and ate in a mess hall. Before they could sit down to a meal, they had to shimmy up and down ropes that the brothers had hung from the rafters. That prepared them to climb trees if a grizzly ever chased them.

Frank and John expected the study to last ten

years. It would take that long, they **hypothesized**, to observe the habits of bears across such a broad territory. (Yellowstone is the largest national park outside of Alaska. It's bigger than the states of Delaware and Rhode Island combined.) Also, the brothers wanted to follow changes in the population over time. That was the only way to learn if, and how, human use of the park was affecting the bears.

The brothers based themselves in Yellowstone from April to November. They usually left after the bears hibernated each winter, although they spent some time studying hibernation. Working in Yellowstone put the Craigheads within an easy drive of Moose, which is about 45 miles from the park's southern entrance. Their families went to the Moose cabins every summer. Frank's family would move there permanently in 1966. The children often helped in the study.

Study team members tagged up to 40 grizzlies a year for tracking. The first step was to sedate the bear. Sometimes they spotted one in the open and felled it with a dart shot from a tranquilizer gun. Other times they captured a bear in a cagelike trap baited with bacon or peanut butter, then sedated it through the trap door. The scientists carried regular guns in case of bear attack. However, they never had to shoot a bear with a bullet during their time in Yellowstone.

Because the drug lasted only about 15 minutes, the scientists had to work quickly. They weighed the bear, measured it, and tattooed it with an identification number. They took plaster imprints of the right front paw and teeth. (A bear's tooth, which grows a new ring each year, indicates its age.) They also tagged the bear's ears with numbered metal tags and an "earring" of colored vinyl streamers. Each bear had its own color combination, making it easy to identify in the field.

Eventually, scientists were able to add a vital step to this process. They put radio collars on the bears, making it possible to track their movements from up to 20 miles away. The invention of the long-range radio collar revolutionized the study of wildlife. Frank Craighead was one of the inventors.

Frank constructing a radio collar in Canyon lab

In the Field

Working with electronics experts, Frank spent a lot of time perfecting the radio collar. It took many field tests to design a bearproof, reliable model.

A radio collar has three key parts: a battery pack, a transmitter, and a loop antenna. These parts allow the collar to broadcast silent, pulsed signals. Scientists use receivers with antennas to pick up the signals and convert them into sound. By turning on their receivers, the Craigheads could "tune into" collared bears. The process is like turning on a radio and tuning into a local station. A tracker could identify an individual bear by counting the pulses or beeps per minute. Each bear had its own number of beeps.

The first grizzly to wear a workable radio collar was Bear Number 40, nicknamed Marian. This shy female bear, or sow, became a favorite of the Craigheads. They radio-collared her from about age 4 to age 12 and tracked the cubs from her three litters.

Marian helped the Craigheads learn about how grizzlies rear their young. Births take place during hibernation, when the mother bear is safe from danger. Most cubs are twins or triplets. They stay with their mothers until age two-and-a-half or three.

Study team members radio-tracking a released grizzly

Getting accurate data about grizzly families was one goal of the study. Another was to learn how much space grizzlies need to find adequate food, mates, and secure dens. All are necessary to keep the population healthy and growing.

The radio collars made it possible to determine a grizzly's territorial range. Canyon lab had a rooftop receiver that picked up distant signals. The signals pointed team members in the general direction of a bear. The researchers then hopped into pickup trucks equipped with midrange receivers. The strength of the beep told them how far away the bear was. A louder beep meant a closer bear! Finally, on foot, they used hand-held receivers to close in.

Although grizzlies have the sheer strength to kill people, they rarely attack unless **provoked**. Still, the Craigheads and their field assistants always used caution. On locating a grizzly, they stayed at least 300 feet away. That put them beyond the animal's "fight or flight" zone, the area in which a bear would be likely to either fight another animal or run from it. If a grizzly did spot them, they did not run away. Running would trigger the bear's **instinct** to chase. Whenever possible, the scientists stood near trees when observing. They could climb a tree to safety, because grizzlies don't climb trees.

Team members watched through binoculars as grizzlies foraged for food, ate, and played. Later, they made notes on the bears' behaviors and plotted their locations on maps.

The study found that grizzlies stay in one home range and share it as long as it offers ample food and mates. The size of the range varies. Females and young bears have modest ranges. Marian's was only about 30 square miles, even when she was foraging for her cubs as well as herself. Male grizzlies, called boars, cover more ground. One tracked boar had a home range of 1,000 square miles! All grizzles wander farthest in autumn. They are fattening up for their winter's sleep.

Whenever a bear left the park's border in search of food, it became fair game for hunters. Often, grizzlies were shot when they went into towns, onto ranches, or onto lands in which hunting was allowed.

Study data proved a crucial point: Very few Yellowstone grizzlies lived only within the park. Most traveled back and forth into at least one of the national forests that surround the park. The Craigheads hoped this fact would encourage the government to limit hunting, logging, and other human uses in those forests. The bears needed protected wilderness. Yellowstone's grizzly population was especially vulnerable, the study found, because birth rates were on a decline.

For 80 years, Yellowstone's grizzlies had been allowed to feed at four garbage dumps in the park. The bears didn't get all their food there, by far. It may seem strange for bears to eat garbage at all. However, as Frank said, "To grizzlies, garbage scraps are as natural as fish, rodents, berries, and roots. When it comes to food, bears don't make a distinction."

In the 1960s, National Park Service officials began to discuss closing the dumps. It was part of an idea to restore national parks to a more natural state. Those discussions became urgent in 1967, after two women were killed by grizzlies in Glacier National Park in Montana. The killings happened on the same night,

Grizzly and cubs at a Yellowstone dump during the study

for no apparent reason. Naturally, the public was terrified. People demanded an explanation of the Park Service's bear management policies.

Soon after the Glacier attacks, Yellowstone got a new superintendent and chief biologist. Those men called for the dumps to be closed quickly. The Craigheads disagreed, and they felt their opinion should count. While they did not work for the Park Service, they had worked closely with the previous superintendent. Study team members had often helped park rangers handle difficult situations with bears. At this point, no one knew more about grizzly behavior—inside and outside of Yellowstone—than the Craigheads.

The brothers urged the new officials not to close all the dumps at once. These were their reasons:

- The dumps were located away from public roads.
- Feeding at the dumps helped keep bears away from Yellowstone's tourists.
- If the bears suddenly found the dumps closed, they would be more likely to forage for food at campgrounds and other tourist sites.
- Bears in campgrounds and public areas are a threat to human safety.
- Bears that cross paths with people often become "beggar bears" and must be relocated or killed.

Frank and John supported their arguments with study data. For example, they noted that 75 percent to 80 percent of the park's 230 or so grizzlies had been observed feeding at the dumps. At that rate, more than 170 bears might be driven into campgrounds by sudden dump closings. The Craigheads argued for a gradual, multiyear reduction of the amount of food at the dumps. That would give the grizzlies time to adjust.

Park officials listened but disagreed. In 1968, the dumps were almost empty of food. Just as Frank and John feared, trouble began.

Both the Craigheads and Park Service officials wanted to keep bears and people apart. Both sides felt tourists should be able to safely enjoy popular Yellowstone sites, such as the regular eruptions of Old Faithful **geyser**. Neither side wished to risk the lives of tourists or bears, but the sides clashed on how to reach those goals.

In fall 1968, Canyon laboratory was **razed**. The brothers brought in their own trailer, but they were soon pressured to move it out of the park.

Worse, starting in 1969, study team members were forbidden to tag or radio-collar grizzlies. Park rangers were under orders to remove existing ear tags and collars whenever possible.

Old Faithful geyser, a prime tourist site in Yellowstone National Park

25

As the brothers had predicted, more bears began coming into campgrounds. Some were trapped and decollared, then relocated or sent to zoos. Some were shot. Park rangers set some snare traps near campgrounds to catch bears.

In summer 1969, grizzlies attacked—but did not kill—two young men and a five-year-old girl at a Yellowstone campground. Park Service leaders held a meeting about the park's bear-management crisis. The Craigheads attended, again speaking out against dump closures. Still, park officials decided to shut another dump that fall. Sadly, it was also a year when berries and pine nuts—important food for bears—were scarce.

The bear Marian, then 11 years old, had fed at one of Yellowstone's dumps all her life. In all the time the Craigheads tracked her, she had never entered a campground. On October 10, she did, with her three **yearlings**. Rangers trapped and relocated two of the youngsters. Three days later, Marian and her last yearling returned. The ranger on duty got between mother and child, a dangerous position.

Naturally, Marian rushed to defend her child. Frank described the scene: "Just short of the ranger, she turned toward her yearling, then pivoted back. . . . The ranger did not hesitate." The park official shot and killed Marian with his .44 Magnum.

Frank mourned the death of Marian, calling her "a grizzly that had adjusted to man perhaps as well as a wild grizzly ever will." He hoped that at least one of her offspring would survive and pass on her genes. The study projected a grimmer fate. If the bear killings continued at increased rates, Yellowstone could lose almost half of its grizzlies.

The Craigheads wanted to follow the remaining bears. To stay in Yellowstone, however, they had to renew their written agreement with the park. It was set to expire. Park officials offered a new one. Under it, the Craigheads would have to submit "all oral and written statements" about their grizzly study to a government agency for approval. The brothers refused to sign. In 1971, "Operation Grizzly Bear" officially ended.

The bear Marian, wearing a radio collar

Frank's Legacy

The Craigheads continued to speak out on behalf of the grizzly. Yellowstone remained in crisis. Between 1968 and 1972, 160 grizzlies died there, and a grizzly killed a tourist near Old Faithful.

The National Academy of Sciences stepped in to **assess** the situation. Academy scientists called the Craighead study "a uniquely rich data bank." The Academy's report said Yellowstone's program wasn't giving the data needed to make sound bear-management policies. At the Academy's urging, the Yellowstone Park Service resumed radio-collaring.

Two key actions came about as a result of the Academy's report. Both actions drew on the Craigheads' ideas, and both have helped America's grizzlies make a comeback. The first was the listing of the grizzly in 1975 as a threatened species under the Endangered Species Act of 1973. The listing outlaws grizzly hunting and helps protect grizzly habitat. The second was the formation of the Interagency Grizzly Bear Committee, which coordinates bear management among federal and state agencies.

Frank wrote a book about the study. *Track of the Grizzly* greatly added to the public understanding of grizzlies and their plight.

In the years following the study, Frank helped develop tiny satellite transmitters to track bird flight. As an avid fisherman, he also worked to save America's rivers from pollution and overuse.

Still, these years were challenging and lonely for Frank. His cabin in Moose burned down, destroying many of his field notes and photographs. He rebuilt the cabin. His beloved wife, Esther, died. Frank and John saw each other less often, since John had returned to his teaching job at the University of Montana.

Frank was delighted to meet and eventually marry Shirley, a woman from New England. She shared his love for the outdoors and was happy to move to Moose.

Grizzly Survival at a Glance

	1961 (Third Year of Study)	2000
Estimated number of grizzlies in Yellowstone National Park	229	280–610*
Estimated number of breeding female grizzlies in Yellowstone	46	90–100**
Visitors to Yellowstone	1,524,088	2,838,233
Hunting of grizzlies on lands adjacent to national parks	Legal	Illegal
Grizzly status	Unprotected	Threatened

*Latest available statistics from Yellowstone National Park, 1996–1997
**Latest available statistics from Interagency Grizzly Bear Committee, 1998

Frank developed Parkinson's disease, an illness of the nervous system. Luckily, the disease progressed slowly. Frank and Shirley enjoyed years of hiking and fishing together, often with Frank's grandchildren. He wrote his last book, *For Everything There Is a Season*, about the **ecosystem** of the Grand Teton-Yellowstone area he knew and loved so well.

Frank didn't just spend his life learning about hawks and owls, rivers and wildflowers, and grizzly bears. With his brother, he made their learning available to everyone through television specials, films, and books. The Craigheads personally trained dozens of wildlife biologists and inspired many more. Christopher Servheen, who directs grizzly recovery for the U.S. Fish and Wildlife Service, has said: "I know so many people who have the same story I have. They got into conservation because of what the Craigheads did."

On its 100th anniversary in 1988, the National Geographic Society honored a handful of scientists for "distinguished contributions to humanity." Frank and John were among the 15 honorees. They shared the stage with such world-class company as Jacques Cousteau, who explored Earth's oceans; Jane Goodall, who researched chimpanzee behavior; and Robert Ballard, who found and raised the remains of the *Titanic*.

Frank Craighead (left) receives the 1988 National Geographic Centennial Award.

In May 2001, the Craigheads received a "Great Bear Stewardship Award." It had special meaning to them because it came from their old **adversary**, the U.S. Department of the Interior, which oversees the National Park Service. Frank attended the award ceremony in his wheelchair. John was there, too. Bear researchers from around the world applauded them.

Frank died peacefully on October 21, 2001. His son Lance, a wildlife scientist, carries on Frank's work through the Craighead Environmental Research Institute, which was founded by Frank. The Institute is building a library and archive in Moose. There, new generations of scientists can learn from Frank's work and venture forth to make their own contributions to the natural world.

Glossary

adversary	opponent
anesthetic	a drug that temporarily causes a total or partial loss of sensation
arid	lacking moisture; dry
assess	to determine the importance of something
ecosystem	a system formed by a community of organisms interacting with their environment
entomologist	a scientist who studies insects and their effects
geyser	a spring that throws heated water and steam into the air
hypothesize	to form a theory in order to investigate its truth
instinct	an inborn tendency; a natural inclination
naturalist	a person who studies nature in the field
provoked	annoyed
raze	to tear down
sedate	make calm through the use of a tranquilizing drug
yearling	an animal between one and two years old